Dear Parent:
Your child's love of reading starts here!

Every child learns to read in a different way and at his or her own speed. Some go back and forth between reading levels and read favorite books again and again. Others read through each level in order. You can help your young reader improve and become more confident by encouraging his or her own interests and abilities. From books your child reads with you to the first books he or she reads alone, there are I Can Read Books for every stage of reading:

SHARED READING
Basic language, word repetition, and whimsical illustrations, ideal for sharing with your emergent reader

BEGINNING READING
Short sentences, familiar words, and simple concepts for children eager to read on their own

READING WITH HELP
Engaging stories, longer sentences, and language play for developing readers

READING ALONE
Complex plots, challenging vocabulary, and high-interest topics for the independent reader

I Can Read Books have introduced children to the joy of reading since 1957. Featuring award-winning authors and illustrators and a fabulous cast of beloved characters, I Can Read Books set the standard for beginning readers.

A lifetime of discovery begins with the magical words **"I Can Read!"**

Visit www.icanread.com for information on enriching your child's reading experience.

Visit www.zonderkidz.com/icanread for more faith-based I Can Read! titles from Zonderkidz.

> "Praise the Lord from the earth,
> you great sea creatures and all of
> the deepest parts of the ocean."
> —*Psalm 148:7*

ZONDERKIDZ

Sea Creatures
Copyright © 2011 by Zonderkidz

An **I Can Read Book**

Requests for information should be addressed to:
Zonderkidz, 3900 *Sparks Drive SE, Grand Rapids, Michigan 49546*

Library of Congress Cataloging-in-Publication Data

Sea creatures.
    p. cm. — (I can read!/made by God)
  ISBN 978-0-310-72183-3 (softcover)
  1. Marine animals—Religious aspects—Christianity—Juvenile literature. 2. Creation—Juvenile literature.
  BT746.S43 2010
  231.7—dc22   2010031104

All Scripture quotations, unless otherwise indicated, are taken from the Holy Bible, *New International Reader's Version*®, *NIrV*®. Copyright © 1996, 1998, by Biblica, Inc.® Used by permission of Zondervan. All rights reserved worldwide.

Any internet addresses (websites, blogs, etc.) and telephone numbers printed in this book are offered as a resource. They are not intended in any way to be or imply an endorsement by Zondervan, nor does Zondervan vouch for the content of these sites and numbers for the life of this book.

No part of this publication may be reproduced, stored in a retrieval system, or transmitted in any form or by any means — electronic, mechanical, photocopy, recording, or any other — except for brief quotations in printed reviews, without the prior permission of the publisher.

I Can Read® and I Can Read Book® are trademarks of HarperCollins Publishers.

Zonderkidz is a trademark of Zondervan.

Editor: Mary Hassinger
Art direction & design: Jody Langley

Printed in China

MADE BY GOD

Sea Creatures

CONTENTS

Jellyfish 6

Sea Horses 12

Sea Turtles 19

Whales 26

God made everything,
and he made it all good.
He made the birds in the sky
and creatures under the sea,
like the …

JELLYFISH!

Jellyfish are not really fish.
They do not have bones.
They are more than 90% water.
Jellyfish look like see-through
umbrellas with long legs
called tentacles.

There are more than
200 kinds of jellyfish.
Some are called:
Lion's mane jellyfish
Box jellyfish.
Jellyfish live in groups called
swarms or blooms.

Jellyfish float in the water.

Some move very quickly.

Jellyfish are in every ocean.

Some live near the top;

others live in the deep sea.

Jellyfish can be huge — 120 feet long!

They can be poisonous.

Some of them sting!

Jellyfish only live

two to six months.

Even though jellyfish do not have brains, hearts, or bones, they are special to God, just like …

11

SEA HORSES!

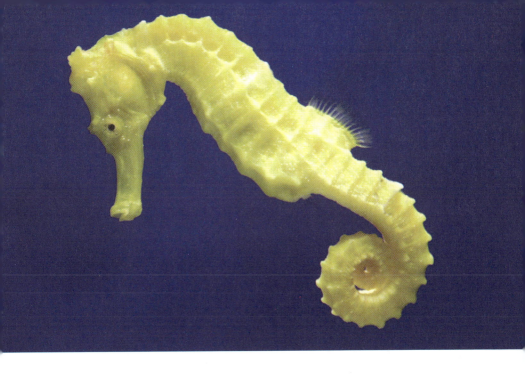

Sea horses are horse-shaped fish.

There are about 35 different kinds.

They live in shallow, warm, tropical water.

Sea horses live one to five years.

They only grow one-half to fourteen inches long.

Sea horses have to eat almost all the time to stay alive. But they do not have teeth or stomachs!

Sea horses use their tails to hold onto sea grass so they can stay still to eat.

They eat plankton and fish eggs.

Sea horses are not good swimmers.
But they have a small fin
on their back
that flutters up to 35 times
in one second.
This helps them move better.

Another special sea horse fact is that father sea horses carry their babies until they are born!

God made many special sea creatures! He also made the amazing …

SEA TURTLES!

There are seven kinds of sea turtles.

Some of them are:

Leatherback

Green turtle

Loggerhead

Kemp's ridley

Some sea turtles are in danger.

People do things that are not safe

for the turtles,

like pollute the water.

Even though sea turtles can

live for 80 years or more,

if people are not careful

sea turtles might all die.

Sea turtles live in all of the oceans, but not in frozen places. They are almost always under water but need to breathe air. When they are swimming, sea turtles eat jellyfish, seaweed, sponges, and algae.

Mother sea turtles come out of the water to lay eggs in the sand. They lay 50 to 100 eggs, bury them in sand, and leave.

When the eggs hatch, the babies run as fast as they can to get to the water.

The leatherback turtle is the largest turtle in the world. It can grow to be seven feet long, three feet across, and 1,500 pounds. Leatherbacks live in groups called bales. They have soft shells.

God made sea turtles so

they cannot pull their heads into

their shells to hide

like other turtles!

God made another undersea creature

so big, they do not have to

hide either … it is the …

WHALES!

Whales are the largest animal on earth.

They are mammals.

This means whales do things like breathe air with their blowholes and have live babies.

There are over 80 kinds of whales.

Some are:

Hector dolphin—the smallest
   at 39 inches,

Blue whale—the largest
   at 100 feet

Humpback whale

Beluga whale

Killer whale (orca)

Whales live in every ocean.
They live in groups
called pods.
They are like a family.

Whales can talk to each other.
They use clicks and pings.
Whales can hear other whales
talk as far away as 100 miles!
Whales can swim fast to get
to each other—30 miles an hour.

God made some underwater creatures very huge.

He made some very small.

No matter the size or shape of his creatures,

God made them all amazing!